PLATO

The Father of Logic

THE LIBRARY OF GREEK PHILOSOPHERS™

PLATO

The Father of Logic

Alex Sniderman

The Rosen Publishing Group, Inc., New York

For Kath, with all the love in the world

Published in 2006 by The Rosen Publishing Group, Inc.
29 East 21st Street, New York, NY 10010

First Edition

Library of Congress Cataloging-in-Publication Data

Sniderman, Alex (Alex Wenley), 1972–
Plato: the father of logic/Alex Sniderman.—1st ed.
  p. cm.—(The library of Greek philosophers)
Includes bibliographical references.
ISBN 1-4042-0498-9 (library binding)
1. Plato. 2. Philosophers—Greece—Biography.
I. Title. II. Series.
B393.S65 2006
184—dc22

2005017131

Printed in China

On the cover: Background: A mosaic from Pompeii illustrates a discussion among philosophers at the Academy, Plato's school. Inset: A sculpture of Plato dating from the Hellenistic period.

CONTENTS

INTRODUCTION

Plato was born into an aristocratic Greek family in 427 BC. He is considered by many scholars and historians to be the father of the study of philosophy. The word "philosophy" is made up of two Greek words: *philos*, or "lover," and *sophia*, which means "wisdom." Accordingly, a philosopher is a lover of wisdom. Plato influenced every philosopher who came after him. He was a devoted pupil of Socrates', the leading philosopher and teacher of the time. Socrates himself was both a primary influence as well as the main character in many of Plato's writings.

The Athens of Plato's youth was the center of Greek culture. Athens was a democracy. Every freeborn male who was the child of two citizen parents

PLATON tres excellent Philosophe, et Prince de Lacademie,
estudia Sous Socrates. il alla en Italie pour entendre les Pita:
goriens, et de la il passa en Ægipte, ou il leut les liures de
Mouyse. il enseigna la Philosophie a Athenes, a Aristote.
il fut le preumier autheur du Dialogue, et de plusieurs
autres Volumes. il mourut Aage de 88 ans.

Se Vendent a Paris chez Iollain rue S¹ Iacque a la Ville de
Cologne

This portrait of Plato was sold in Paris, France. Translated, it reads,
"Plato, an excellent philosopher and the prince of the Academy, studied
under Socrates. He went to Italy to attend some theatrical performances
and from there, he went to Egypt. He taught Aristotle philosophy in
Athens and he was the author of the *Dialogues* and many other volumes.

became a citizen and had the right to vote. Theater and drama were also important in Athens. Many of the plays written during Plato's time are still studied and performed today.

In addition to its political and artistic advancements, all during Plato's youth, Athens was fighting the Peloponnesian War (431–404 BC) with Sparta. The war had its origins more than fifty years earlier, when a group of Greek city-states (including Athens, Chios, Samos, and Lesbos) held back an assault by the Persians in 480 BC. These Greek city-states formed the Delian League in 478 BC and built a navy to keep the Persians out. Athens was the most powerful member, with the strongest navy, and the league came to be referred to by many historians as the Athenian Empire. The Peloponnesian War specifically began when the Athenian navy prevented the Spartan ally Corinth from invading Corcyra, and attacked the Corinthian colony of Potidaea. Athens also refused to trade with another Spartan ally, Megara, effectively crippling Megara's economy. Athens was eventually defeated when Plato was about twenty-three years old. Plato and others blamed Athens's defeat on the city's focus on politics and culture. Eventually, the Spartan way of life would inspire Plato to formulate his thoughts on what he believed to be the ideal way of

life. He would write about this in his famous work *The Republic.*

Plato distrusted the Athenian democracy of his childhood and believed that a civilized society functioned best when governed by a small group of wise men that would advise and make laws for the good of all. During this time, Athens was still a city with a strict class system, enslaving close to 100,000 people. Many people who were part of the upper classes believed that Athens gave the poor and uneducated too much power by granting every citizen the right to vote.

Plato's writings differ from those of other philosophers in that he wrote in the form of dialogues, or discussions between two or more characters. Most philosophers present their ideas and theories in essays in which they introduce and build upon their ideas in a series of paragraphs. Plato's dialogues featured characters discussing a variety of philosophical issues including mathematics, science, ethics, death, and the universe.

In late antiquity, Plato was thought to be the author of thirty-six dialogues, most of which have been passed on through time in something of their original form. Scholars today believe that approximately twenty-seven of these are genuine. Plato was also credited with thirteen letters. Of these, contemporary

This terra-cotta vessel (circa 550–530 BC) is decorated with images of women making cloth. The two women on the left of this olive oil container are using handheld spindles to spin wool into a basket. In the center of the pot, two slightly smaller women are shown working with a weaving loom. In Plato's time, the production of textiles and fabrics, an extremely important task, was relegated to women only.

investigators think only three are genuine. The most important is the seventh, which contains important biographical material about Plato's early years and his political activities in Sicily. Most accounts of Plato's life and its relationship to his thought are based on this letter. Since the nineteenth century, scholars have divided Plato's works into three periods: early, middle, and late. In the early dialogues, they argue, he sketches a portrait of his teacher Socrates and defends his legacy. In the middle dialogues, he begins to present his own ideas, especially the theory of forms. In the late period, he criticizes the shortcomings of this

theory and offers a corrected view. Some investigators, however, question this evaluation. As a result, it no longer commands universal assent. Nonetheless, it remains the dominant interpretation of his works.

Plato's best-known and arguably most important dialogue is *The Republic. The Republic*, written in the first half of the fourth century BC, is divided into ten books discussing some of Plato's most important ideas. Books 1 through 5 discuss Plato's vision of the perfect government and his definition of justice. Books 6 and 7 discuss what a philosopher is and introduce Plato's theory of ideas or forms. Books 8 and 9 of *The Republic* discuss three practical forms of government and the positive and negative revisions of each. The main idea of Plato's work as a whole was to present the question "How best should a person live?" Socrates' role in Plato's dialogues is often one in which he questions people about what they claim to know. Socrates asks pointed questions that force others to rethink their beliefs, often causing them to doubt what they believed at the beginning.

In 387 BC, after several years of traveling to cities in both Africa and Italy, Plato spent the rest of his life teaching and writing at the Academy, the school he founded just outside Athens. Plato remained there until the end of his life in 347 BC.

1 SON OF ATHENS

Not much is known about Plato's day-to-day life. Most of the information concerning Plato is derived from his philosophical writings. However, it is certain that he was born into a rich and powerful Athens family about 427 BC. He was named Aristocles at birth in honor of his grandfather. During his early career as a wrestler (probably in his late teens or early twenties), he was given the nickname Plato (the Greek word for "flat" or "broad") in recognition of his broad shoulders. It is not known who first gave him the name, but he was known as Plato for the rest of his life.

THE ATHENIAN CITY-STATE

Athens was the largest polis, or city-state, in ancient Greece. The city-states of

Pictured above is a modern reconstruction of Athens's famous Acropolis, featuring all of its most famous buildings. Shown here are the Temple of Athena Nike, the Pinakotheke, the Propylaea, the Parthenon, the Erechtheum, and the House of the Arrephoroi.

ancient Greece were large metropolitan centers, which were part of the Greek nation. They had separate governments, laws, military, and cultural traditions. The word "metropolitan" comes from the word "metropolis," from the Greek *metera*, meaning "mother," and *polis*, meaning "town." The term "metropolis" refers to any large town or urban place that is the cultural or economic center of its surrounding region. The metropolitan area of Athens also included Attica, a surrounding area outside the city.

Greek city-states had three different types of governments. The first was autocracy, in which one person, such as a king, had absolute power over the entire population. A second type of government for city-states was oligarchy, in which a small group of the rich and powerful made policy decisions for all. However, the Greeks are best remembered for inventing democracy, in which each citizen (defined as males who had been born in the city-state) had the right to vote on policy.

Only about 40,000 people out of the total population of 300,000 to 350,000 Athenians were considered citizens. For example, women were completely excluded. Metics, free men who had immigrated from other countries or other parts of Greece in search of work, were not allowed to vote. However,

they contributed to the economy through their employment and paid taxes to the city-state as did Athenian citizens. The enormous slave class, which made up close to one-third of the city's population, was not paid for its work. The slaves did not pay taxes and were unable to participate in the political process.

Athens's location close to the sea made it a center for trade. Many Greek goods, including wines, pottery, and olive oil, were exported. Because much of Greece's land was mountainous, and the soil conditions were poor, the Greeks imported most of their food. Since the Greek soil made it impossible to grow the large amounts of grain that were needed by the population, grain was imported from the coastal region of the Black Sea (consisting of Turkey, Romania, Russia, Georgia, Bulgaria, and Ukraine). Other goods in short supply were meat, fish, and wood (for building ships), as well as slaves, who were often captured soldiers.

PLATO'S FAMILY AND HOME LIFE

Plato's mother was related to Solon (638–558 BC), a legendary Greek statesman. Solon was one of the seven sages who were famous for sayings such as

A typical ancient Greek family having a meal is depicted in this marble relief. Wealthy families such as Plato's probably ate fish (which was very abundant because Greece is almost completely surrounded by water), bread prepared by the women in the house, olives, and fruits and vegetables during dinnertime. It was common for people to eat their meals while lying on their sides, as depicted above.

"Know thyself," and "Nothing in excess"—two phrases still common today. Plato's father, Ariston, came from the family of Codrus, the last king of Athens. Two other relatives were members of the notorious Thirty Tyrants. These were thirty upper-class men who ruled Athens after the Peloponnesian War.

Historians believe that because Plato's family was wealthy and powerful, it probably had several slaves to help handle daily duties around the house.

Because Athens had no sewer system, wealthy families had private wells. Less fortunate Athenians (or their slaves) had to visit a spring for freshwater and carry the water home in large ceramic jugs.

Homes of wealthier Athenians (like Plato's family) were usually built of stone. The poorer Athenians made their homes from mud brick. These dwellings were easy prey for thieves and burglars, who were known as wall-diggers.

A typical Athenian man went to the agora, or marketplace, to buy food and other necessities for his household each morning. Women, unless they were forced to work outside the home to help support their families, were not allowed to venture out on their own. In wealthier homes, women were typically in charge of managing the slaves. Slaves took care of the smaller children as well as the housework.

THE GREEK GODS AND RELIGION

The Greek religion was polytheistic, meaning that Greeks worshipped many different gods. This contrasts with religions such as Christianity, Islam, and Judaism, which are monotheistic, or centered on worship of one god. The Greek gods were said to live at the top of Mount Olympus, the highest mountain in Greece.

This image shows an ancient stone sculpture commemorating the Greek goddess Artemis, who is seen standing in the center of the twelve Olympian gods. Although most frequently identified by scholars of Greek mythology as the goddess of hunting, Artemis was also associated with childbirth, wild animals, and the moon.

The Greeks considered the twelve Olympian gods (Zeus, Poseidon, Hera, Artemis, Hermes, Aphrodite, Apollo, Demeter, Hephaestus, Ares, Athena, and Hestia) to be the most important. Nonetheless, many other gods (such as Dionysus, the god of wine) were honored by the Greeks. The Olympian gods were a large, quarrelsome family, headed by Zeus. Zeus was ruler of the heavens and the most powerful of the gods. He was responsible for justice, frequently settling quarrels with a hurled lightning bolt. Zeus's wife, Hera, was the goddess of marriage, and his brother Poseidon was god of the oceans. Some gods symbolized human emotions; Aphrodite, for example, was the goddess of love. The Greek gods were a lively bunch. They were constantly mixing themselves up in feuds and love affairs with each other—sometimes even with humans.

The ancient Greeks also believed that certain people known as oracles had the ability to see into the future and understand things no other person could. The most famous Greek oracle was the Oracle of Delphi. The temple at Delphi was built as a shrine to Apollo, the god of music. Apollo was believed to speak through the oracle. Seekers of truth would regularly journey to Delphi with questions, and the oracle would dispense answers and advice for a fee.

The Olympian Gods	
Zeus	Ruler of the gods; god of the heavens
Poseidon	God of the sea
Apollo	God of the sun, light, medicine, and music
Hephaestus	God of fire
Ares	God of war
Hermes	Messenger of the gods
Hera	Wife of Zeus; goddess of marriage
Artemis	Goddess of the hunt, forest, wildlife, and the moon
Aphrodite	Goddess of love
Athena	Goddess of wisdom
Hestia	Goddess of the home
Demeter	Goddess of agriculture

The most powerful Greek god, Zeus, is shown here on his colossal throne inside the temple that is named after him, the Temple of Zeus. The temple is located in Olympia, which is on the west coast of Greece. The first Olympic Games were held here in honor of Zeus in 776 BC. In the ancient Olympic Games, only men who spoke Greek were allowed to compete, and there were significantly fewer events than there are today.

ANCIENT GREEK ARTS: DRAMA, ART, AND ARCHITECTURE

One of the ways the Athenians honored their gods was by going to the theater to see plays. The city set aside two days for its citizens to see these dramatic performances. The elaborate spectacles were at the

This is an architectural detail from an actor's coffin. Sculpted into the marble are two tragic masks. A pair of masks—one illustrating a sad or tragic face, the other depicting comedy—have long been used as symbols representing Greek theater. Because each actor played many roles, different masks were worn to represent a wide array of emotions.

center of an important religious festival held in honor of Dionysus. They were attended by up to 14,000 people at a time. Plays were performed on a circle of ground called the orchestra, which roughly translates to "the dancing place." Greek plays had only two or three principal characters, and the action was commented on and sung about by a group of singers and dancers known as a chorus.

Comedy and tragedy, the two varieties of drama invented by the ancient Greeks, are still considered the cornerstones of modern theater. Drama and poetry were in many ways treated as sports. There were great festivals and contests that went on for days, and at the end, a winner was given a prize. Plato himself participated in several poetry contests before deciding to focus his energies on philosophy.

The arts of ancient Greece are still appreciated and studied today—especially sculpture and pottery. Greek pottery illustrated everything from scenes of everyday ancient life to religious or historical events. Luckily, a fair amount of Greek pottery has survived. Sculpture was also very important. Many statues and monuments were created in honor of gods, famous heroes, or statesmen.

The architecture of ancient Greece featured many formidable and lasting monuments to commemorate

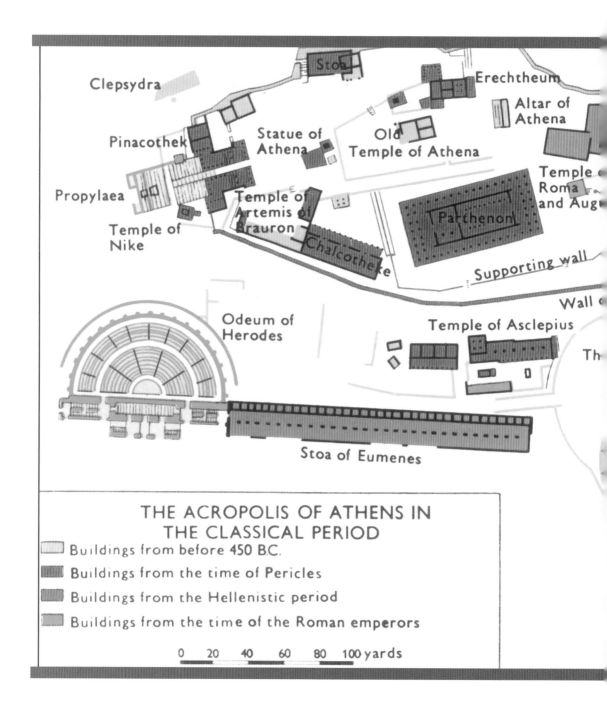

Clepsydra

Stoa

Erechtheum

Altar of
Athena

Pinacothek

Statue of
Athena

Old
Temple of Athena

Temple
Roma
and Aug

Propylaea

Temple of
Artemis of
Brauron

Parthenon

Temple of
Nike

Chalcotheke

Supporting wall

Wall

Odeum of
Herodes

Temple of Asclepius

Th

Stoa of Eumenes

THE ACROPOLIS OF ATHENS IN
THE CLASSICAL PERIOD

Buildings from before 450 B.C.

Buildings from the time of Pericles

Buildings from the Hellenistic period

Buildings from the time of the Roman emperors

0   20   40   60   80   100 yards

the gods and their civilization. Of all the Greek arts, examples of architecture have survived most intact. The most famous Greek monument is probably the Acropolis, a collection of temples built to honor the gods of Olympus.

One of the most famous monuments in Athens is the Parthenon, which is seen above in this aerial view. At present, the Museum of the Parthenon is said to be the second-most important museum in Greece after the National Archaeology Museum, which is also located in Athens. This architectural plan shows all of the buildings on the Acropolis of Athens during the Classical period.

On the highest point of the Acropolis stands the Parthenon, a temple honoring Athena, the Greek goddess of wisdom for whom the city of Athens was named. Ruins of the Acropolis are still standing.

PLATO'S EDUCATION AND EARLY LIFE

Though not much factual information is known about Plato's early life, his education probably consisted of studying with private tutors in his home, learning how to read, write, and play music. When boys in ancient Greece were older, they were given physical training and exercise in the gymnasium, which set the stage for military training.

The first great Greek civilization was that of the Mycenaeans (1600–1100 BC), whose times were recounted in the work of the famous blind Greek poet named Homer. Historians believe Homer lived sometime in the eighth century BC, about 400 years before Plato. The epic poetry of Homer's *Iliad* and *Odyssey* recounts the deeds of legendary heroes Achilles and Odysseus. These stories, which remain classics of Greek literature and civilization, were essential reading for young Greeks.

The Olympic Games originated in Greece. Though Plato was a highly regarded wrestler, he never

This type of pottery, known as black figure, is a common artifact from ancient Greece. This vase depicts the ship of Odysseus, Homer's famous adventurer from the classic literary work *Odyssey*. To make this sort of pottery, a red clay structure was covered with a black varnish into which drawings were incised with a sharp-edged tool. Art historians believe this technique probably dates from around 700 BC.

competed in the Olympics. Historians have never been able to determine why this was. He did, however, win first place in the Isthmian Games two different times, and he was quite famous for his skill in the ring.

Though Plato's family background suggested a career in Athenian politics, two events turned him from this path. After the defeat of Athens in the Peloponnesian War, the Spartans appointed a thirty-man board (including Plato's mother's cousin Critias and his uncle Charmides) to help govern the city. They promised a policy of reform and asked their nephew Plato to become involved. Plato eagerly waited to see what they would do. Contrary to their stated aims, his kinsmen tried to consolidate power by murdering

What Is Philosophy?

Philosophy is the study or pursuit of wisdom. The ancient Greeks were the fathers of what is called Western philosophy, a system of thought used to make sense of the world. It is known as Western philosophy because the ideas originated in Europe. Western philosophy encompasses many different disciplines, including science, religion, politics, and ethics.

Several civilizations produced great thinkers prior to the ancient Greeks, including the Hebrews, Arabs, and Egyptians. However, before the Greek philosophers began their work, there were no experiments or measured tests, simply the conclusions of each philosopher. For example, a philosopher would consider a question or problem (such as why olives grew in one place better than in another), decide upon a solution, and declare it to be the truth without any proof to support his decision. Many things that could not be explained were thought to be the results of some supernatural force.

Plato is an especially significant philosopher because he was the first of the ancient Greek thinkers whose works survived in a condition similar to their original form and not as fragments. Plato's teacher Socrates was brilliant and had a deep influence on Plato and all those who came after him, but he never wrote down any of his own philosophy. Most of what historians know of Socrates' work is derived from Plato's writings.

their opponents and confiscating their property. In all, they killed about 1,500 men. Plato was horrified and withdrew. After the thirty were overthrown, he observed the moderation of the restored democracy toward the defeated oligarchs, and he again grew hopeful about entering politics. His hopes were dashed, however, when they executed his beloved teacher, Socrates. After considering all this and continuing to be disappointed with events, Plato gave up his political ambitions. He realized that reform was impossible without fundamental and almost miraculous changes. Upon hearing Socrates, Plato never wavered from his desire to teach and study philosophy.

PLATO'S CONTEMPORARIES

Plato came to his conclusions based on the ideas of those who came before him, building on Socrates' method of questioning and refuting those past philosophers with whom he disagreed. Three philosophers whose work Plato took issue with were Protagoras, Theodorus, and Heraclitus.

Protagoras believed that knowledge was something relative, or unique to each person, because each person's experiences and opinions were different. For

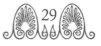

example, one person might huddle under blankets saying that a 50-degree-Fahrenheit (10-degree-Celsius) day was freezing, while on that same day, another person might decide to wear very little clothing and complain about the heat. According to Protagoras, both conclusions were true. Protagoras is well known for saying "Man is the measure of all things." In other words, each person's individual experience teaches him to make judgments about the world.

Another contemporary of Plato's was the mathematician and philosopher Theodorus. In the field of mathematics, Theodorus is best known for his work

Heraclitus (circa 535–475 BC) is shown in this seventeenth-century French painting. Heraclitus of Ephesus was one of the many contemporaries of Plato's with whom he philosophically disagreed. The laurel leaf (more commonly known as the bay leaf) crown on his head is a symbol of notoriety. Heraclitus, who was born into an aristocratic family, wrote an important book called *On Nature*, which he dedicated to the Temple of Artemis. However, it is not known whether or not he taught at an actual school, as did Plato.

with square roots. Philosophically, Theodorus believed that understanding the world meant experiencing it through the five senses of smell, sight, taste, touch, and hearing.

The ideas Protagoras and Theodorus believed in were completely opposed to Plato's. Plato's theory of forms (which were absolute, unchanging, and perfect) clashed with Protagoras's theory of relativism as well as with Theodorus's belief that experience equals knowledge. Plato's ideas addressed ultimate truths that were seen as valid in the same way for every person.

Plato also disagreed completely with the philosopher Heraclitus. Heraclitus believed that the world was in a state of constant flux, or change. He believed people's ideas altered as they learned new information and had different life experiences. Accordingly, his work is similar to both Protagoras's belief in relativism and Theodorus's idea of individual experience. According to Plato's dialogue the *Cratylus*, Heraclitus stated, "You cannot go into the same water [of a river] twice." Heraclitus is putting forth the idea that the water, wildlife, and plants in the river will change as the river flows, and as such, nothing in life will be exactly the same when a person crosses it.

Plato strongly disagreed with Heraclitus. He argued that if everything was in a state of constant change,

This is a bronze sculpture of Leonidas, the king of Sparta. This imposing and regal monument graces the ancient battlefield at Thermopylae, where Leonidas was killed in 480 BC. Though the Spartans had little chance of victory in the attack on the warring Persians, they held their ground. Ultimately, every single warrior in the 300-plus Spartan army was killed along with Leonidas. After their success, the Persians marched on to Athens.

no one would be able to talk to each other because the actual names of people and objects—the entire language itself—would be constantly changing. Each person would only be able to understand language

individually. Hence, communication would be nearly impossible, as no one could understand anyone else. Plato struggled to disprove these ideas and create his own theory of knowledge and truth in response. Eventually, he came to his theory of forms.

SPARTA

When Plato was a young man, Athens was defeated by the southern Greek city-state of Sparta in the Peloponnesian War. Spartan society was militarized because they constantly feared that the more numerous slaves would revolt. For example, when Spartan boys were seven years old, they were taken from their families and sent to live in barracks where they would begin military training. As in Athens, the number of slaves (known in Sparta as Helots) greatly outnumbered the free citizens. The Spartan citizens treated Helots with cruelty. They forced Helots to serve in the Spartan army but denied them any rights in the government.

When Athens was defeated by Sparta, the Spartans tore down the city walls and installed a pro-Spartan oligarchy in which a group of thirty rich and powerful Athenians governed the polis. Among these thirty Athenians were Plato's relatives Critias and Charmides. The Thirty Tyrants, as they

Socrates and the Socratic Method

Socrates was born in Athens around the year 470 BC. Historians believe he was the son of a midwife and a stonemason, but it is impossible to be certain due to a lack of proper documentation and historical sources. Socrates' method of teaching, which was revolutionary at the time, is still in use today. The Socratic method, as it is known, is used to direct a student toward deducing an answer by presenting the student with a series of questions. For example, a teacher would ask students to provide the definition of justice. Perhaps a student would respond with the answer that justice is a decision by a court of law. The teacher would then ask students if court cases were always decided in a just or fair way. The students might answer, no, not in every single case. This contradiction would lead the group to examine other situations and ideas and how each related to justice. Ideally, the students and teacher would ultimately be able to eliminate conflicting ideas until a single definition of justice could be agreed upon.

were known, often executed their enemies and forced many to flee the city in fear. Many enemies of the Thirty Tyrants who escaped Athens tried to raise armies to drive them out and restore democratic rule in the city. In 403 BC, the democratic opposition managed to run the Thirty Tyrants out of town. As

This wall painting shows Socrates, the famous mentor of Plato. Socrates was part of the same intellectual movement that had created an interest in the Sophists' teachings. Plato's *Euthyphro, Crito, Phaedo,* and *Apology* were all heavily influenced by his studies with Socrates. These would become known as his early works.

a result, the Spartans realized it would be better to reconcile these two with each other. They made them swear to a truce, and restored the democracy.

Despite his connections to the Thirty Tyrants and other famous statesmen, Plato gave up his political ambitions. The cruelty with which the Thirty Tyrants governed Athens completely disgusted him. But this disappointment didn't really matter. Plato had already found something more attractive than political power. By 408 BC, he had become a steady companion of the great philosopher Socrates.

SOCRATES AND THE SOPHISTS

Although Socrates was a stonemason by trade, and he had family (a wife and three sons) to support, he is thought to have spent most of his time engaging in philosophical discussions in the agora, or marketplace, of Athens. He was not at all interested in money and did not charge for his teaching. He was only concerned with the study of philosophy. Socrates was an opponent of the Sophists, teachers who traveled through Greece teaching classes for a fee. The Sophists' philosophy stated that the important thing in life was getting what you wanted and persuading others to give it to you. In contrast, Socrates thought the role of knowledge was to learn how to be a good person. He felt that the Sophists ignored this, which he considered to be the most important concept within philosophical thought.

SOCRATES THE PHILOSOPHER

When Plato met Socrates, Plato believed he had finally found a subject, philosophy, to which he could devote his life. He became Socrates' most famous student and constant companion for the next nine years. Plato tried to learn all he could from Socrates. As a result, Socrates would become his most influential teacher.

Socrates believed that gaining knowledge about oneself and the world was key to self-improvement. Although he was humble about the limits of his own knowledge, he believed that it was possible to live the life of a good person through a process of continual questioning of issues. Socrates became famous in Athens for his abilities to expose people's lack of knowledge. As a result of his skill of debate and intellect, people crowded around him to hear what he had to say.

THE TRIAL OF SOCRATES

After years spent teaching in the streets of Athens, in 399 BC, Socrates was formally charged with corrupting the youth of Athens. Those in power believed that Socrates and the Sophists' constant questioning of traditional values was influencing the youth of Athens in the wrong way. Socrates vigorously defended himself against this charge. He argued that he was nothing more than a seeker of truth. Despite Socrates' protests, he was sentenced to death.

Plato took his teacher's death very hard. He realized that as a friend of Socrates', he was also in danger. As a result, he left Athens shortly thereafter.

2 PLATO AND SOCRATES

Socrates' work had angered so many Athenians that a number of his followers, including Plato, left the city in fear of their lives. Plato's first stop was a neighboring territory called Megara. Although Megara was only twenty miles (thirty-two kilometers) away from Athens, Plato remained there safely for the next three years. Also living there at the time was his friend Euclid and several other Socratic followers who had fled Athens.

Unlike the majority of philosophers, Plato wrote his work in the form of dialogues. Most philosophers write essays, in which the author puts forth his ideas in a series of paragraphs, building point upon point for maximum effect. However, Plato's work was structured much more like drama. In his dialogues, two or more characters discussed issues back

This manuscript page of Plato's *The Dialogues* was dedicated to Lorenzo the Magnificent circa 1480. Lorenzo the Magnificent was a historian from Florence, Italy, who was the head of the Medici family. They were great patrons of the arts and literature. Cosimo de'Medici, the grandfather of Lorenzo, had many important literary works in his great library, including some pieces from Plato.

and forth, eventually coming to a final conclusion. Plato's dialogues often feature Socrates questioning the views of other participants until he established that they were not entirely correct.

WHO WERE PLATO AND SOCRATES?

It's not entirely known whether the views expressed by Socrates as a character are truly his or merely Plato's thoughts relayed through his mouth. Because Socrates is featured throughout many of Plato's dialogues, it's easy to conclude that the ideas Plato discusses are those of Socrates. Historians admit that it's impossible to know whether Plato's assertions came from Socrates or if Plato used Socrates' character as a vehicle to put forth his own ideas. The truth is probably somewhere in the middle.

In his dialogues, Plato presents Socrates as both an example of an honest person after whom others should follow as well as a provocative thinker who would go to almost any length to make his opponents admit they are wrong. Because of the lack of historical information on the lives of both Plato and Socrates, it's impossible to determine what these two men were like in real life. The only conclusions that can be drawn about Socrates come from Plato's work and the work of other writers.

The most important of these were the playwright Aristophanes, who mocked Socrates in a powerful satire called *The Clouds*, and Socrates' former pupil Xenophon, who wrote a defense of his teacher, reminiscences about the Socratic circle, and a few brief dialogues.

Plato's first works are based on trying to prove that Socrates' search for truth was the best way to live—the way that all people should live. Plato found it very

The Academy of Science is one of three classical Temples of the Mind on the Odos Panepistimiu. The Odos (meaning street) Panepistimiu is in downtown Athens. The building, home to the University of Athens, is flanked by statues of Plato and Socrates.

difficult to face the idea that although Socrates had lived what Plato considered an honest life, he ended up being put to death by his government. He probably used the character of Socrates to get across his own ideas as well as those of Socrates'.

APOLOGY AND THE TRIAL OF SOCRATES

One of Plato's first works is *Apology*, in which Plato reconstructs Socrates' entire defense during his trial. This is the most accurate record of Socrates using his questioning method in action. Throughout *Apology*, Socrates addresses the jury and prosecutors in the courtroom.

Socrates' defense tactic in *Apology* was to try and prove to the court that instead of being guilty of corruption, he was actually providing a public service to Athenians by helping them find the truth, or more specifically, aiding them to come to a realization of what they really knew. In *Apology*, Socrates recalls his friend Chaerephon's trip to the oracle at Delphi. Chaerephon asked the oracle who was the wisest mortal, or human being. The oracle responded that "no man is wiser" than Socrates. This completely shocked Socrates and compelled him to undertake the mission of finding a man who was wiser than he was.

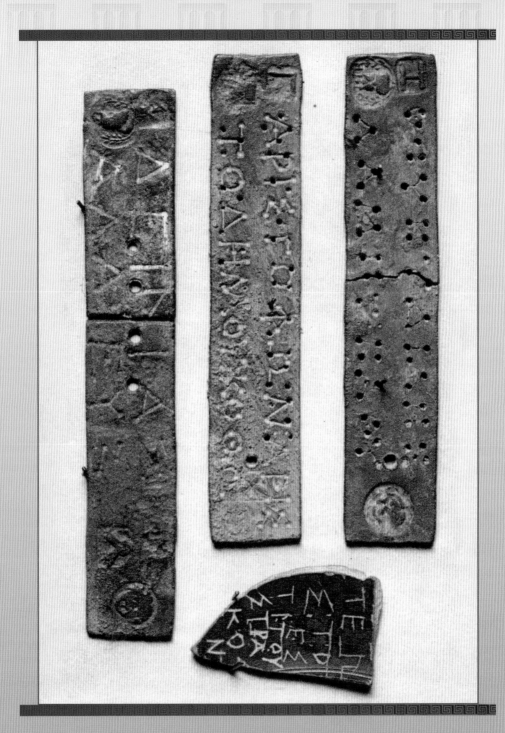

In the trial of Socrates, the members of the jury would have cast their votes by having the judge punch holes in a piece of soft clay. The juror's tickets (*above*) were used to track points awarded for statements made during a trial. This inventive means of calculation is the forerunner to trial notes that exist today. In Greek, jurors were called *dikastai*.

Since the Oracle of Delphi was believed to be infallible, or unable to make a mistake, Socrates could not deny her statement. However, Socrates still thought of himself as ignorant. He believed that human beings cannot truly know anything worthwhile. Socrates felt that the only knowledge or wisdom he truly had was that he freely admitted what he did not know. Socrates decided the only fair test would be to try and find someone wiser.

After he met with many men (for example, the young priest Euthyphro, who was known for being wise) and was unable to find anyone who could stand up to his intense questioning, he ultimately decided he was only wise in one small way. As he stated in *Apology*, "when I do not know; neither do I think I know." In other words, although he did not feel particularly wise, Socrates was aware of the limits of his knowledge and he freely admitted it.

Many of Socrates' opponents refused to admit that they might not be wise until Socrates was able to prove it. In *Apology*, Socrates told the jury that he felt he was chosen for the mission of showing people the true depth of their knowledge. As he stated:

The god has placed me in the city. I never cease to rouse [excite, stir up] each and

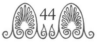

every one of you, to persuade and reproach you all day long and everywhere I find myself in your company.

Socrates saw himself much like a priest who takes a vow of poverty in order to spend his time ministering to others. Believing that the most important thing a person could do is find the truth, in *Apology*, Socrates noted that "the unexamined life is not worth living." He felt that through this process of questioning he would be able to help people find the true way to live. As he continued:

> I go around seeking out anyone, citizen or stranger, whom I think wise. Then if I do not think he is, I come to the assistance of the god and show him that he is not wise.

Socrates defended himself against the charge that he was corrupting young people. He told the court that he never forced his ideas or beliefs on anyone. Instead, he simply searched for the truth and anyone who wanted to follow him was welcome to do so.

SOCRATES' INFLUENCE ON YOUNG ATHENIANS

Athens was a center of culture and intellect. Accordingly, many wealthy Athenians became patrons of the arts and encouraged their children to become educated. Because Plato, as a child of the upper class, did not need to earn his living, he became a student of Socrates'. Since these young people did not need to work, they had the opportunity to spend their time in other ways. Some chose to spend it studying philosophy. They watched and learned from Socrates' teaching methods. As a result, many Athenian students began to use these methods to question their elders. They did so in much the same way that Socrates challenged his opponents. In many cases, they found that their elders would eventually demonstrate their own ignorance just as Socrates' opponents had. Naturally, the students' elders became angry because they felt their children were using their educations against them.

Socrates believed that the real problem was that the elders merely did not want to be questioned. Many of them thought that being queried by their children eroded their status as parents or authority

figures. Socrates pointed out in *Apology* that those who were questioned "are angry, not with themselves but with me." Socrates felt that the anger these people felt at being taken to task by their children led them to view him as a scapegoat. They came to the conclusion that Socrates, as the instigator, was the problem. They concluded that if Socrates was disposed of, they would not have to face the fact that they may not be as smart as they would like to think.

Although Plato's *Apology* indicates that Socrates defended himself admirably, the court still found him guilty of corrupting the young. As a result, he was sentenced to death. As was the Athenian custom, the accused person was allowed to propose an alternative to the punishment offered by the prosecutor. Socrates reasoned that because his aims had been to make Athenians aware of the truth about their lives, and to make them work at being better people, he was actually performing a public service. Socrates thought that instead of a death penalty for performing good work, he should receive free meals for the rest of his life. One last option Socrates brought forth was the possibility of paying a fine. However, as he admitted that he had no wealth to speak of, he could only pay a fine of one mina, which amounted to about twenty-five dollars.

The court voted for the last time, and the verdict to put Socrates to death stood unchanged. As written in Plato's *Apology*, Socrates reacted to the decision by stating, "It is not hard to avoid death . . . it is much more difficult to avoid wickedness." He went on to predict that killing him would not destroy his ideas. Socrates told the court that his followers and fellow philosophers would come forward in his place and continue his work. As he stated in *Apology*, "You are wrong if you believe that by killing people you will prevent anyone from reproaching you for not living in the right way." He continued, saying that he did not fear death and looked forward to the next world.

Socrates' follower and friend Crito pleaded with Socrates to escape Athens. However, Socrates soundly refused. Although he disagreed with the court's decision, Socrates felt that to escape would be breaking the law. Also, such an act would damage the integrity of the honest life he had lived. Even if the court was wrong, he was willing to abide by the decision because he felt that to disobey the law would be worse than death. Accordingly, he willingly drank the poisonous hemlock he was given. He died surrounded by many of his followers, including Plato. Eventually, Plato would write about his mentor's death in his work *Phaedo*.

Plato and Pythagoras

Aside from Socrates, one of the most important influences on Plato's work was Pythagoras of Samos, a philosopher, musician, and mathematician. Like Socrates, Pythagoras did not write down any of his ideas. Another similarity between the two is that they each had an enthusiastic group of followers. Pythagoras's followers lived together as a group in their own settlement for many years after the death of their leader.

Pythagoras believed that numbers were the key to learning the truth about the world. A famous saying attributed to Pythagoras is "All

This sixteenth-century fresco shows Plato with Pythagoras. Historians often refer to Pythagoras as one of the first true mathematicians. Born in about 569 BC in Ionia, Pythagoras left few written documents because the society to which he belonged followed a strict code of secrecy. As a result, a lot about him is often disputed among scholars.

is number." Pythagoras believed that the world is literally constructed from numbers, that numbers are used in the same way that one would use building blocks. In other words, he felt that numbers could explain the entire world (which also included the senses). Integral to his discoveries, numbers provided the basis for the explanation of relationships in various disciplines, including mathematics and music. Pythagoras was the first person to identify the reason certain musical notes sound good together. As a mathematician, he is most known for the Pythagorean theorem. This famous theorem states that the square of the hypotenuse (the side opposite the right angle of a right triangle) is equal to the sum of the squares of the other two sides.

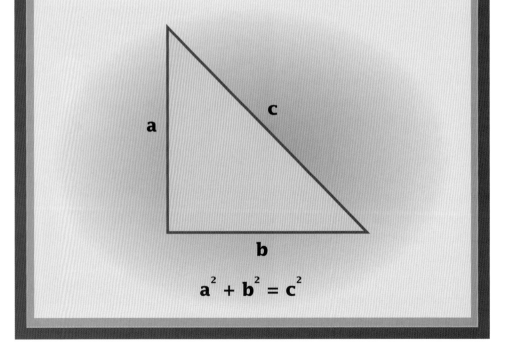

$$a^2 + b^2 = c^2$$

PLATO'S FELLOW PHILOSOPHER ARCHYTUS

During his travels away from Athens, Plato spent time with a group of Pythagoreans who had settled in Tarentum, in the south of Italy. There, he met a philosopher named Archytus, who would become a good friend. At the time, Archytus and Plato were both about forty years old. Plato was very impressed with the fact that Archytus was equally as involved in politics as he was in philosophy. Archytus gave Plato a concrete example of how a person could be both a philosopher and a ruler—an ideal Plato would try to realize for the rest of his life.

EARLY DIALOGUES: *EUTHYPHRO*, *CRITO*, AND *PHAEDO*

In addition to *Apology*, three other dialogues Plato wrote—*Euthyphro*, *Crito*, and *Phaedo*—discuss the last days of Socrates' life. In each dialogue, Plato further explores Socrates' ideas, using his trial and death to show Socrates' integrity as an honest person who was in search of the truth. Socrates paid the ultimate price for the truth—his life—which he gave without complaint and with great dignity. In two of the four

These two pages from Euclid's *Elements* (circa 300 BC) is one of the oldest surviving texts of mathematics. Housed in the library of the Vatican in Italy, these two pages are part of a hugely influential collection of ancient manuscripts and documents that would have otherwise been lost. These two pages are from Book 1 Proposition 47, the Pythagorean Theorem. Euclid of Alexandria (325–265 BC) helped preserve some of the most vital ideas of ancient Greek philosophers and mathematicians.

early dialogues—*Apology* and *Euthyphro*—Plato gives Socrates the role of a smart aleck who is aware that he won't be getting the answers he desires from the person he's questioning. Socrates is not mean-spirited, only disappointed in his inability to get the response he's after. He is merely trying to make people think, as he states in *Apology*.

EUTHYPHRO

Euthyphro features Socrates trying to discover and understand the nature of piety, or being true and respectful of the gods. In the dialogue, Plato places Socrates in the company of Euthyphro, a young priest, who, despite his standing as a religious leader, is unable to give Socrates a true definition of piety.

Plato sets the scene with Socrates making his way to his trial. On the way to court, Socrates meets Euthyphro who is involved in a different trial. Euthyphro tells Socrates he is trying his own father for murder. A servant in his father's house killed one of the family's slaves. His father tied up the killer and left him in a ditch while he sent for instructions from the priest about what to do with the killer. While the messenger was gone, the killer died of exposure. Euthyphro's actions angered many Athenians. They

Only remnants remain of Plato's famous work *Phaedo*. Seen above are the delicate remains of what historians say is the oldest classical manuscript in existence. These two pages of text each contain twenty-two lines of text and are written on papyrus. Papyrus first became common as a writing material in adient Egypt. Made from a plant, papyrus is similar to paper.

said it was impious, or against the will of the gods, to prosecute one's own father.

Plato leads Socrates to engage Euthyphro in a discussion of the nature of piety. Socrates believes that, as a priest, Euthyphro has special insight into the true definition of piety. Euthyphro tells Socrates that "what is dear to the gods is pious, what is not is impious." Plato has Socrates point out to Euthyphro that

the Greek gods are not perfect beings. In many religions, such as Christianity, Islam, and Judaism, it is believed that God is perfect. However, the Olympians fought frequently among themselves, had many petty jealousies, and sometimes engaged in romantic affairs with human beings.

By pointing out the faults of the gods, Plato shows that because the Olympian gods disagree over many things, what one god believed to be pious, another might not agree with. This means that the definition of piety that Euthyphro gives Socrates does not hold true. Euthyphro then brings up the idea that if the gods love something, they love it because of its piety; in other words, it is not pious just because they love it.

At this point, Euthyphro is drawn in to Socrates' web of questioning and begins searching for any way out of the situation. Socrates states that if he could prove to the court that he had acquired real knowledge of piety, the court might have mercy on him. As such, he might be able to "escape [prosecutor] Meletus' indictment by showing him that [he] had acquired wisdom in divine matters from Euthyphro." Euthyphro eventually tells Socrates he doesn't have the time to give him a true definition of piety, and heads to his trial. Unfortunately, Socrates is forced to do the same.

As in *Apology*, in *Euthyphro*, Plato allows Socrates to present a logical argument about his subject, which his opponent is not able to contradict. In both dialogues, Socrates' opponents come to their own conclusions without paying much attention to Socrates' exposure of the flaws in their thinking. In allowing Socrates to put forth ideas that contradict those of men like Euthyphro the priest and Meletus the prosecutor (who were thought to be wise), Plato seems to be saying that many people in powerful positions may not be willing to listen to ideas that contradict their own—no matter how much sense these ideas make.

CRITO

Plato's depiction of Socrates in *Crito* is a marked contrast of how Socrates appears in *Apology*. In *Apology*, in which Socrates suggests that his punishment be free meals for life in return for his service to Athens, he is presented as thoughtful, wise, and willing to die even though he believes himself to be innocent—all just to prove his point that by honestly following the laws of Athens, he will remain innocent and his opponents guilty.

Crito takes place in Socrates' prison cell as he awaits execution. In this dialogue, Plato illustrates

Socrates' honesty and integrity by having him refuse the option of an easy escape from Athens and, hence, from death. In an unusual twist of fate, Socrates' execution is put off for a month due to a religious mission in which a Greek ship was sent on a return journey to the island of Delos. During the voyage, no executions are allowed to take place. At the time of Crito and Socrates' conversation, the ship is returning to Athens. It is during this time that Crito tries to convince Socrates to make use of his last chance to escape his death sentence, but Socrates would hear nothing of it.

Crito tells Socrates, "I do not think that what you are doing is right, to give up your life when you can save it," but Socrates soundly refuses Crito's invitation to escape. Socrates expresses to Crito that "One should never do wrong in return, nor injure any man, whatever injury one has suffered at his hands." Socrates feels that trying to escape his punishment would be ignoring all the laws of Athens. Accordingly, he tells Crito that if people begin ignoring laws, society would crumble. Though he calmly refuses to believe that what he has done is wrong, Socrates does not deny the Athenian court's right to order that he be put to death.

By presenting Socrates as a man who'd rather die than go against the laws of his homeland, Plato once again depicts Socrates' strength of character in the face of unjust opposition. The Socrates Plato presents in *Crito* refuses to think of himself or his own safety. Instead, he is only concerned with living an honest and just life, even if it comes at the expense of his own life. He states that running away would "strengthen the conviction of the jury that they passed the right sentence" on Socrates—that to flee would be to admit guilt. Crito finally realizes that his friend's resolve is absolute and that no matter what he says, he will not be able to persuade Socrates to save his life by leaving Athens to avoid his death.

PHAEDO

In *Phaedo*, Socrates continues to philosophize with his students and friends up to the end of his life. Despite his difficult manner when questioning people, the Socrates portrayed by Plato in *Phaedo* is a wise gentleman who goes to his death with no regrets or sadness. Of course, those around him are terribly upset. Socrates shows such peace in the face of death that even the officer who comes to administer the poison to him is moved by his

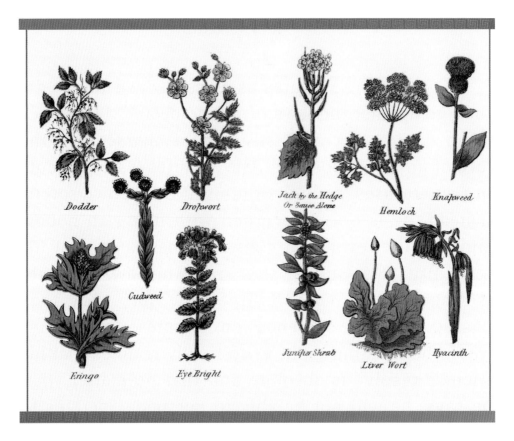

Pictured above are images of herbs and flowers, among them hemlock, the poisonous plant that notoriously killed Socrates, Plato's most influential mentor. Some of the other plants featured in this 1869 book include dropwort, cudweed, juniper, liverwort, and hyacinth.

dignity. The officer tells Socrates that he is "the noblest, the gentlest, and the best man who has ever come here." Socrates takes the cup of poison, drinks it, and dies. His followers openly weep around him.

3 | THE PHILOSOPHER

After Plato's first works in which his goal was to depict Socrates in the best possible light, Plato began to explore his own theory of knowledge. Building on Pythagoras's idea of a perfect world of numbers, Plato believed that the world was divided in two parts: the world that can be perceived through our senses, and a more perfect world of ideas which, in principle, human beings can only reach through the mind. He began working with this idea in *Phaedo* and continued it in *The Republic*.

Plato called these perfect ideas forms. He believed that in their daily lives, humans do not directly experience forms. Instead, they experience visible, material objects. Plato suggested that these ordinary objects are imperfect copies of the perfect forms. Philosophy students of

Plato's were taught that the objects of the world are not completely unique and that each object has various elements that can be categorized in various groupings. For example, there are categories, or forms, for objects, such as animals, and there are forms for concepts, such as beauty and justice. Plato believed that the forms cause objects to be what they are. For example, the form of a lion makes a lion the animal that we perceive through our senses. Though objects, such as a lion, can die, and what we may consider beautiful may change, the forms never change. They are eternal and remain perfect. Socrates states in *The Republic* that people who cannot see the forms are like people who are dreaming but think they are awake. Only the philosopher can know the truth about ordinary experience because a philosopher can see the dream for what it is.

THE CAVE

In Book 7 of *The Republic*, Plato explains his idea that normal reality is like a dream by using an example of people who are forced to live their entire lives chained together inside a cave and unable to move:

> Picture human beings living in an underground dwelling like a cave, with a long

entrance open to the light, as wide as the cave. They are there from childhood, with chains on their legs and their necks so that they stay where they are and can only see in front of them, unable to turn their heads because of the fetters. Light comes from a fire which is burning higher up and some

This sixteenth-century painting shows people chained up inside the cave that Plato discusses in *The Republic*. Unlike what the Flemish artist depicted above, the men in *The Republic* are chained with their faces toward the wall. This way, their backs are to the fire and they are not able to see reality, but rather, the shadows of reality.

way behind them; and also higher up, between the first and the prisoners, there is a road along which a low wall is built, like the screen in front of puppeteers above which they show their puppets.

In the cave, people are chained together in a line, unable to move, or even turn their heads. A fire behind them casts shadows of puppets in front of the fire. Since the prisoners cannot see anything except the shadows, they believe that there is nothing else. They do not even know that these are shadows since they have never seen the puppets or the fire behind them. In constructing this allegory, Plato is saying that people who do not understand the forms are living in a sort of prison of the mind. In this prison, what the prisoners think of as the real world of experience is only a projection of something else. The shadows are to the puppets as the visible objects of ordinary experience are to the forms.

However, the world of the cave is more complex than this since there are two sets of images and originals in it. Socrates writes of a prisoner who is freed from his bonds and leaves the cave. On his way out, he sees and experiences many things. First, he sees the puppets and the fire that create the shadows on

the wall of the cave. With difficulty, the prisoner is able to leave the cave and enter into the light of day. At first, he is blinded by the brightness of the light. Slowly, as his eyes become accustomed to the sun, he is able to distinguish reflections and the shadows of things outside of the cave. Ultimately, he becomes aware of his surroundings and the sun that provides light. He also recognizes that the puppets are copies of the things outside of the cave.

Once the prisoner takes all of this in, he begins to understand that the objects outside of the cave are the source of the things inside the cave. The puppets are modeled on the objects outside of the cave, and the shadows are shaped like the puppets. Now the prisoner can understand that just as the shadows in the cave are images of the puppets, so everything in the cave is like an image of what is outside of the cave. (The shadows, then, are not even like visible objects, but more like images on a television or movie screen. People would be just like the prisoners if they watched a movie and thought it was reality instead of images of and stories created about the world.) In this way, the world inside the cave represents the visible world and the world outside the cave represents the world of ideas.

The fire that allows the prisoner to see the shadows and the puppets inside the cave represents the sun in the world outside the cave. In the same way, the sun shining outside the cave represents the object that allows people to see the forms.

THE FORM OF THE GOOD

Plato states in *The Republic*, "What provides truth to the things known and gives the power to the one who knows is the idea of the good." Truth is like light in that it explains what we can understand. In other words, what Plato is defining as the good is the source of our ability to comprehend. To know what is good or what is best would be to know why things in the world are the way they are. For example, in *Euthyphro*, Plato has Socrates ask Euthyphro to define piety, but the young priest is unable to do so. Plato asserts that if Euthyphro truly understood the form of the good, he would have no trouble giving Socrates an exact definition of piety. According to Plato, the form of the good is the basis for understanding all other ideas.

To know and understand the form of the good provides one with the tools to find the truth in every idea and object. Being able to do so is also the key to the ability to live an honest life. However, Plato also warns that while both knowledge and truth are effects of the good, they should not be confused with the

Helois, the sun god, was mentioned in Plato's allegory of the cave. In ancient Greek mythology, Helios (who is said to have been from the island of Rhodes) was associated with fertility. It was believed that Helios saw and heard everything that took place on Earth. Because of this, it was common for ancient Greeks to invoke the name of the sun god when they needed to take an oath.

form of the good. According to Plato, that would be like confusing the sun's light with the sun itself. Sunlight is only a product of the sun, just as knowledge and truth are products of the good. The good is the underlying basic idea that makes all other knowledge possible.

Plato believed that all human beings are born with the capacity to understand the form of the good. Plato states in Book 7 of *The Republic* that "this power is in the soul of each" person. However, just as the prisoner's journey out of the cave is a difficult and painful one, so is the effort to understand the good. Instead of needing to be educated or instructed on what is true, Plato felt that people needed to have their minds turned toward the good, since this is the source of all truth and knowledge. In other words,

being instructed about what is true is not enough. What is really needed is a complete change of the soul "until it is able to endure looking at that which is, and the brightest part of that which is. And we affirm that this is the good." Plato is suggesting that everyone has the ability to understand the world by turning toward the good. If human beings are able to face the good, they will always be able to understand what truth is. This understanding would enable people to not only "see" the forms that stand behind the visible world, but to understand why the forms themselves are what they are.

PLATO'S FIRST TRIP TO SYRACUSE

During his travels to the island of Sicily, Plato became acquainted with Dion, the brother-in-law of the ruler of Syracuse. Syracuse's king Dionysius I was a great soldier and military leader who built his kingdom into a military powerhouse by using brilliant strategy to crush his opponents. An admirer of the arts and philosophy, Dionysius I was well known for his own poetry and drama. One of his plays won an award at an Athenian festival, though the rumor was that the prize was only given to prevent Dionysius I from attacking Plato's home city.

Dion convinced Plato that Dionysius I might have a place in his court for a philosopher. Plato was eager to give the position a try. Unfortunately for Plato, Dionysius I, like the Athenians who tried Socrates in court, did not take kindly to Plato's use of the Socratic method of questioning. The two men disagreed about many ideas and ultimately, their disagreements ended when Dionysius I accused Plato of being an old fool. Plato shot back that Dionysius I was acting like a tyrant by asking him to come to Syracuse and instruct him in philosophy only to ignore all Plato's teaching and advice. In a fit of anger, Dionysius I had Plato thrown in jail and deported from Syracuse on a Spartan ship. Dionysius I told the ship's captain to sell Plato as a slave in the market on the island of Aegina.

In an amazing turn of luck, Plato managed to get away from this situation almost completely unscathed. When Plato was on the auction block at the market, a friend and fellow philosopher named Anniceris recognized him and purchased him. He immediately set Plato free and sent him back to Athens.

THE PHILOSOPHER KING IDEAL

Scholars think that the time that Plato spent with Dionysius I led him to think about what kind of a society

A nineteenth-century map of the city of Syracuse shows the main port from which Plato would have departed when he narrowly escaped being sold as a slave. Very little is known about ancient Greek ships. They were not very durable since they were built out of wood.

would be best and how this ideal society should be governed. Plato concluded that this ideal society would best be governed by a capable leader who had a complete understanding of the form of the good. In much of *The Republic*, Plato discusses what the perfect society would entail and a way of living that would provide the good life to all of its inhabitants. In *The Republic*, Plato states, "unless the philosophers rule as kings or those now called kings and chiefs genuinely and adequately philosophize . . . there will be no rest from ills for the cities . . . nor I think for human kind."

Dionysius I is a bad ruler in Plato's ideal society. According to Plato, to rule means to set things in order according to what is best. This requires an understanding of the good. Although the ruler of Syracuse was a great military leader and could command large numbers of people, he did not truly understand the form of the good. When Plato pointed this out to the king,

Dionysius I was unable to tolerate Plato's criticism of him. Plato believed his philosopher king would have an understanding of the form of the good and that he would not feel threatened by someone trying to prove him wrong.

4 THE TEACHER

In 387 BC, upon his return to Athens after nearly being sold into slavery in Aegina, Plato founded a school known as the Academy just outside Athens. Except for two additional visits to Sicily, he would spend the rest of his life there. He devoted his time at the school to studying, teaching, and writing. After Socrates' trial, Plato believed that the only way to improve the situation would be for him to train young people to be statesmen. During this time, Plato wrote down his views on issues ranging from how to build the perfect society to his ideas on love and the soul.

THE ACADEMY

Plato's Academy was located in a grove of trees just outside the walls of Athens. The area, known as the Grove of Academe,

The above engraving on wood depicts Plato and his many students in the lush gardens of the Academy. Originally a suburb of Athens, the site of Plato's famous school had been inhabited since prehistoric times. After Plato's death, the school continued until AD 526, when the Roman emperor Justinian decided to close it. At present, the site is an often-visited public park.

was originally developed as a park. It had been the site of many religious festivals honoring the goddess Athena. The walled grounds, which were planted with olive trees, were also home to a large number of statues and temples. Plato owned a small garden on the property. It was here that he began giving his classes.

Plato's Academy trained philosophers and thinkers— most notably Aristotle—for more than 900 years

until AD 529, when Roman emperor Justinian closed it. Justinian claimed that the Academy and its teachers taught paganism, which contrasted with his Christian faith. Plato taught classes in addition to supervising the other teachers. Science, mathematics, philosophy, and government were taught. There was a gymnasium on the property where students would engage in gymnastics and exercise, including wrestling, Plato's favorite sport. Plato accepted the enrollment of all who applied, including women, which surprised the historians who discovered several women's names on class lists found in the Academy's ruins.

Plato taught at the Academy for forty years until his death in 347 BC. Because the teachers set school policy as a group, no one person had absolute power. This arrangement encouraged cooperation and allowed the Academy to change with the times. Scholars think that Plato composed many of his dialogues during his time at the Academy, including *The Republic*.

ARISTOTLE

Aristotle, Plato's most famous pupil, came to the Academy at the age of seventeen in 367 BC. He was from Macedonia in the northeast part of what is now

This is a tenth-century Latin translation of Plato's theories on cosmology—a branch of astronomy that pertains to the order of the universe. Executed in the fifth century, this treatise resides among many other important copies of text dating from the Middle Ages that eventually became part of the Vatican library in Rome.

Greece. His father, Nichomachus, was Macedonian king Amyntas III's personal physician. Aristotle arrived while Plato was away visiting the court of Dionysius II in Sicily. Aristotle stayed at the Academy for twenty years, teaching there after his studies were completed. After Plato died in 347 BC, Aristotle left Athens for twelve years.

Aristotle traveled first to Asia Minor in present-day Turkey and the island of Lesbos, where he tutored students and studied local plants and animals. In 342 BC, King Philip II of Macedonia hired Aristotle to tutor

This illustration from a manuscript dating from the Italian Renaissance depicts a scholarly Aristotle hard at work. This ancient text is part of the treasured collection of manuscripts that once belonged to the emperor of Vienna, Maximilian I. Though Maximilian was not well known for his intellect, he was an ardent collector of rare books and manuscripts.

Alexander, his son and heir to the Macedonian throne. Aristotle taught Alexander grammar, politics, and literature with special attention paid to the Greek classics by Homer, *Iliad* and *Odyssey*, in addition to philosophy.

In 335 BC, Aristotle returned to Athens and founded a school of his own known as the Lyceum. With

In this fourteenth-century illuminated manuscript (on vellum, a fine-grained calfskin), Aristotle is giving his pupil Alexander the Great a lesson in morals. Alexander III of Macedon was tutored by Aristotle until his father, King Philip II of Macedonia, was killed and his young son had to take over.

generous financial contributions from Alexander, who ruled Macedonia after Philip's death in 336 BC, Aristotle built enormous collections of both plant and animal specimens as well as a large library of maps and manuscripts at the Lyceum.

Although Aristotle greatly admired Plato, many of Aristotle's original ideas and theories were in opposition to those of Plato. For example, Aristotle readily disagreed with Plato's theory of the forms. Instead, he believed the world was observable through our senses of smell, taste, touch, sight, and sound. According to Aristotle, the only way to learn about the world was to study it

Greatest expansion of the empi[re]
Areas dependent on Alexander

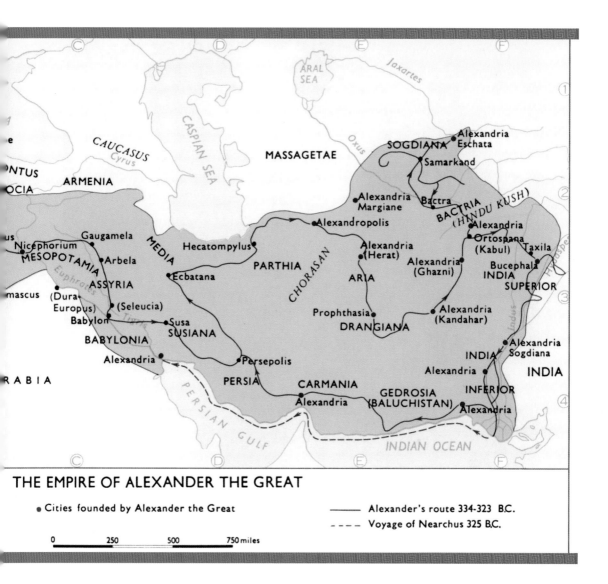

THE EMPIRE OF ALEXANDER THE GREAT

- Cities founded by Alexander the Great
- ——— Alexander's route 334-323 B.C.
- ---- Voyage of Nearchus 325 B.C.

0   250   500   750 miles

The above map illustrates the immense stretches of land that were valiantly conquered by Alexander the Great after he took over the throne from his father. The inset at left depicts Alexander on his trusty horse, Bucephalus. After Alexander's early death, his great empire—which started in the Mediterranean and spread all the way to India—disintegrated.

Aristotle's Logic

Aside from his scientific work, Aristotle is best remembered for creating a system of reasoning known as logic. Logic describes the rules for drawing valid conclusions from already established premises. Aristotle thought that these rules could all be expressed as syllogisms. For example:

All candy is sweet.
Chocolate is candy.
Therefore, chocolate is sweet.

Aristotle's logic is an early ancestor of the scientific method, the system of steps that is used when undertaking scientific experiments and research. Aristotle's idea of drawing conclusions from sources or ideas observed in the real world gave humankind research tools to learn about the world. His pioneering helped make possible a lot of important work in medicine, philosophy, and science that continues today.

scientifically, using a methodology that focused on using reason and scientific experiments. Aristotle made great strides in the sciences. The method for categorizing plants and animals still used by biologists today is based on Aristotle's original idea.

PLATO'S UTOPIA

Plato based many of his ideas of a perfect society, or utopia, on Sparta, the city-state that conquered and ruled Athens during Plato's young adulthood. The entire Spartan society was geared toward war and defending itself against enemies, and Plato's utopia shared many of these properties.

In Plato's perfect society, the guardians or military class did not have any personal possessions. Everything was held collectively by the state or the entire society. Plato conceived of a strict system of education and training that would eventually produce what he believed to be the best kind of ruler for his perfect society.

Like the Spartans, Plato believed that all children should be taken from their families and educated as a group. Plato reasoned that raising children apart from parents would instill in them the idea that the state was assuming the parental role as opposed to their biological mother and father. According to Plato, this would make the children loyal to the state and teach them that protecting it was their responsibility.

If the idea of separating children from their parents seems strange, it may have seemed fairly natural to Plato. This is because Plato's mother did not stay with Plato's birth father, but instead married another man.

As a result, Plato lived in several different homes as a child, and the traditional roles of parent and child did not mean much to him. Coupled with the influence of the Spartans who ruled Athens, Plato may have felt that separating children and parents was the only practical way to ensure that society would continue.

However, Plato's ideas differed from those of the Spartans in one very important way: he believed men and women were equal. This was a fairly radical idea for the time, but Plato practiced it in his own life, such as by teaching females as well as males at the Academy.

Plato believed that all people were born with certain abilities and that it was up to the leaders of state to decide whether people would be best employed as farmers, businesspeople, soldiers, or rulers. Plato's utopia put its citizens through a rigorous educational program, separating them according to ability. Plato created a myth that explained his system of grouping people. His idea was that Earth was the true mother of all people. He believed that people were fashioned from certain metals, which would indicate their position in society.

He presented this idea of being born into a position in *The Republic,* stating that "in fashioning those of you who would be competent to rule," the gods "mixed gold in at their birth; this is why they are most honored;

This is a stunning gold mask of Agamemnon, one of the main characters in Homer's epic poem *Iliad*. Agamemnon was the son of Atreus and the brother of Menelaus. According to Homer, he was the king of Mycenae. However, in later historical and literary texts from ancient Greece, Agamemnon was said to be the king of Argos. During the Trojan War, he was a valiant leader of the Greek forces.

in auxiliaries [the military], silver; and iron and bronze in the farmers and the other craftsmen." In other words, people who were made primarily of gold, for example, would become the rulers, or guardians of

the society; those made mostly from silver would be soldiers; and those made with mostly bronze and iron would be farmers and businesspeople.

Plato also stated that the social position of a child's parents did not automatically determine the position of the child. He wrote in *The Republic* that sometimes "a silver child will be born from a golden parent, a golden child from a silver parent, and similarly all the others from each other." Plato leaves room for every person in his utopia to rise or fall in status to his or her truest potential as a member of the society.

EDUCATION IN PLATO'S UTOPIA

In Plato's utopia, education would be initially concentrated in two areas: music and gymnastics. The study of music would not be just learning to play an instrument or sing; it would also involve poetry. The music and poetry would focus on the ideas of justice and the ability to be a good citizen of the state. The music would be military marches, which Plato believed helped promote courage and moderation. Drama and poetry that did not help create the right virtues and outlook in the city's guardians would be banned. Gymnastics would be studied to promote health and well being as well as preparation for military training.

Plato is shown charming the wild animals with the enticing sounds of his music in this miniature painting that accompanied a sixteenth-century Indian poem by author Nizami. The script is in Persian. The existence of such a rich variety of texts and illustrations devoted to Plato—which come from all around the world—indicates the fundamental impact he had on philosophers, scientists, and scholars.

When young people reached the age of twenty, the students who showed the most academic promise would be selected to continue their educations. Meanwhile, those who did not would be trained to work as craftspeople, farmers, and businesspeople. Their role would be to support the entire society. For the next ten years, those who continued their studies would concentrate on the study of science and mathematics, including astronomy, geometry, and general arithmetic.

After ten years of science and math, the best students again would be separated into two groups based on their academic performance. Those who excelled would become politicians and would rule the state upon completing their educations. The others would be sent into careers in the military. The group of future politicians would study philosophy for the next five years, followed by fifteen years of education in government. Schooling would last until the students reached the age of fifty. Plato felt that they would be the only people whose capabilities could be relied upon to rule justly. In Plato's works, he doesn't indicate how many of these chosen philosopher-rulers would govern in his perfect state, but from this group, one supreme ruler would be chosen. This person would become what Plato termed the philosopher king.

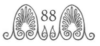

LIFE IN PLATO'S UTOPIA

These chosen men and women lived together in a dormitory-style arrangement. Marriage was not permitted among these chosen rulers, although romantic love was not banned. Marriage, Plato felt, was better left to those who were unworthy to rule—in other words, the farmers, businesspeople, and craftspeople who supported the society. Even in a marriage among the lower classes, children would be separated from their parents. Plato felt

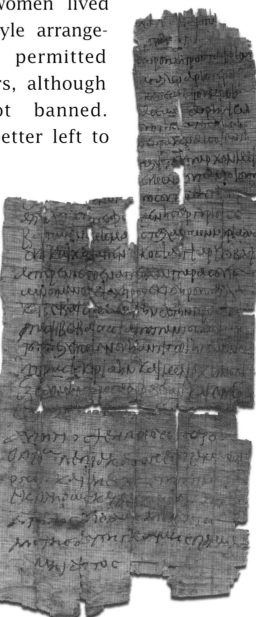

The remnants of an invoice on papyrus dating from AD 383 document the sale of a donkey. Donkeys were an important means of transport in ancient Greek culture.

that forcing his philosopher-rulers to live without personal attachments or possessions would make them impossible to corrupt, since their loyalty would be first and foremost to the state.

People would be fed, clothed, and protected from harm, but the chief focus was keeping the society going. There would not be much advancement in culture or the arts, since all forms of culture that did not support or glorify the state would be banned. In Plato's utopia, the society would be well defended and self-sustaining, but many rights and privileges of individuals would be ignored in favor of the good of the society as a whole.

DIONYSIUS II

In 367 BC, Plato's old friend Dion informed him that Dionysius I, the first ruler Plato tried to mold into his ideal philosopher king, had recently died. His son Dionysius II had ascended to the throne. The boy's father had been so paranoid about his son stealing power that he imprisoned Dionysius II for most of his childhood. The younger Dionysius spent his days doing carpentry projects, completely excluded from his father's court.

Dion believed that a ruler who had not been exposed to the politics of the court was the ideal person to be molded into a true philosopher king. Dion begged Plato to make a return journey to Italy. Plato, who was eager to test his ideas about the makings of an ideal ruler in the real world, consented and made the journey to Syracuse.

Unfortunately for Plato and Dion, their initial ideas about Dionysius II could not have been more wrong. The new king was surrounded by many of the same courtiers who had made his father's court such a dangerous place for both of them. Because of Dionysius II's lack of experience, he was easily controlled by these people. At the courtiers' urging, Dionysius II accused both Dion and Plato of treason. The young ruler banished his uncle Dion from the kingdom and forced Plato to stay in Syracuse. Luckily for Plato, he was once again rescued by friends and returned to the safety of Athens and the Academy, where Dion was waiting for him.

Dionysius II, who was extremely upset that Plato had escaped Syracuse, kept sending word to Athens that he wanted Plato to return. The young king was in no position to explore any of Plato's ideas about utopia because Carthage was waging war against Syracuse in an attempt to conquer Italy. However, Dionysius II enjoyed the philosophical discussions and came to regard Plato as a sort

Dion (with his arm outstretched) is presenting Plato (seated) at the court of the tyrant Dionysius in Syracuse. Plato would later find himself at the center of an intense family feud that would continue over the course of several decades. Ultimately, he would voyage to Syracuse, end up imprisoned there, and then be exiled because of his friendship with Dion.

of father figure. Dionysius II attempted to blackmail Plato into returning to Syracuse by threatening to seize all of Dion's possessions if Plato refused to return.

Eventually, Plato agreed to go back and help his friend. He sailed for Syracuse for a third time in 361 BC. When Plato arrived, Dionysius II paid little attention

to Plato but still refused to allow him to leave Syracuse. Once again, Plato had to rely on friends for an escape back to Athens. After a time, Dion returned to Syracuse, dethroned his nephew, and ruled Syracuse until he was assassinated in 354 BC.

Plato's inability to make either Dionysius I or Dionysius II into his ideal philosopher king made him rethink his ideas of the ideal society. However, many of the aspects of Plato's utopia are present in government systems today. In the twentieth century, communism and fascism exhibited many of the characteristics of Plato's utopia, including a strong government with a primary ruler who was supported by a group of political advisers, state-run defense, agriculture and business programs, and the practice of banning any art that criticized the state. The existence of these systems proves that Plato's ideas about a perfect society could work in the real world, although one might not want to live in such a society.

PLATONIC LOVE

In the dialogue *The Symposium* (389 BC), Plato took on what many scholars, philosophers, and artists consider to be the most complex subject of all—love. *The Symposium* takes place at a party in Athens where

many of the city's cultural aristocracy (including Socrates) are gathered to celebrate Agathon's drama award for a tragedy he wrote. In the end of *The Symposium*, Plato has Socrates tell his colleagues that love is what draws us upward toward the forms. Plato believed that love was the soul's motivation toward goodness. According to Plato, physical or romantic attraction to another person was the lowest form of love. Plato believed that the impulse to love another unselfishly is the greatest act of which human souls are capable. The concept of loving someone in a non-romantic way has come to be known as platonic love.

THE SOUL

According to Plato, the soul of a human being is the core of a person's character. Plato believed that the soul was divided into three parts: the appetites, spirit, and mind. The mind prevented desires of both the appetites and spirit from overwhelming the soul. Without the mind to oversee it, the appetites would seek only passion and pleasure. According to Plato, these are the least honorable desires. The spirit represents all emotions, which drives a person to show courage and do great deeds. When a person's spirit is unbalanced, he or

In this fifteenth-century illustration from a copy of Dante's *The Divine Comedy*, Plato, who is standing to the far left, is shown pointing to a soul ascending to a star in the sky. Plato, who is purposely drawn to resemble a medieval astrologer, believed that the soul was immortal and that it was as much of a living thing as the human body.

she can easily become overconfident and make serious blunders, which can lead to terrible consequences—even death.

In his dialogue *The Phaedrus*, Plato discussed the ability to control the objectionable appetites that can lead a person toward making an error. He stated that "happiness depends on self-control." Many characters in Greek mythology exhibited character defects known as tragic flaws, which ultimately led them to make deadly mistakes. An example is the myth of Daedalus and Icarus, a father and son who were imprisoned in a tower on the island of Crete. Because the king monitored all ships leaving the island, Daedalus could not escape by sea. In search

The infamous myth of Icarus and his father, Deadalus, is one of the most well-known greek myths. Icarus, who was young and impetuous, did not have the patience to listen to his father, hence, he flew too close to the sun, and the rays of the heat melted the wax that held together his feathered wings.

of a way out, he constructed two pairs of wings from feathers and wax. He then instructed Icarus how to use them, telling him not to fly too close to the sun because the wax would melt and cause the wings to fall apart. However, Icarus did not listen to his father. When he flew too close to the sun, his wings fell apart, and he fell into the sea and drowned. The myth of Icarus is an illustration of what can happen to a person who allows appetites for pleasure to overwhelm self-control.

PLATO'S LAST DIALOGUE

In his last dialogue, known as the *Laws*, Plato once again tackled the idea of building a society as he had in *The Republic*. However, this time, he was less interested in a perfect society than one that would function in the real world. Socrates does not appear as a character in the *Laws*. Instead, Plato substituted the Athenian Stranger, who functions as Socrates did in previous dialogues by asking questions and pointing out the faulty arguments of others as he cleverly puts forth his own point of view. After he finished the *Laws*, in 347 BC, Plato died at the age of eighty-one. He was buried at the Academy. Like his teacher Socrates, Plato dedicated his entire life to the pursuit of truth and wisdom. He was a philosopher to the end.

CONCLUSION

Perhaps the reason Plato's work has lived on for 2,000 years is that the questions he asked have continued

This is a page from a seventeenth-century French translation of Plato's seminal dialogue *The Banquet*. Along with *The Republic*, it is among Plato's most widely read works. The story, which is also known as *The Symposium*, was written around 360 BC. It is about a philosophical debate on two types of love. A distinction is made between "common" love, which is identified with youthful lust and physical attraction, and "heavenly" love, which is based on maturity, intellect, and virtue. Heavenly love is considered to be more noble.

to make people think. St. Augustine, an early Christian priest and scholar, believed that Plato's world of the ideal forms represented heaven. St. Augustine thought that by understanding the true nature of forms, a person could have a greater understanding of God.

Other questions Plato raised, such as how to create the perfect society, continue to create discussion. Although living in Plato's utopia might not be particularly appealing to most people, the question of how to create the best type of society is still one upon which human beings are unable to agree. Plato's devotion to philosophy and the search for truth above all else keep his work alive. The fundamental questions he asked are riddles that humanity will face for many generations to come.

TIMELINE

427 BC	Plato is born in Athens.
399 BC	Socrates is tried and sentenced to death. Plato leaves Athens for Megara, Italy, and North Africa for twelve years.
388 BC	Plato makes his first visit to Syracuse in the court of Dionysius I. Dionysius attempts to have Plato sold into slavery on the island of Aegina, but Plato is rescued by a friend and returned to Athens.
387 BC	Plato founds the Academy in the Grove of Academe outside the city of Athens. The Academy continues for 900 years until Roman emperor Justinian closes all philosophy schools in AD 529.
367 BC	Plato returns to Syracuse at the urging of Dion to tutor the young king Dionysius II.
361–360 BC	Plato visits the court of Dionysius II of Syracuse for the last time.
347 BC	Plato dies in Athens, at the age of eighty-one. He is buried at the Academy.

GLOSSARY

Academy Plato's school at the outskirts of Athens; the Academy is considered the first university.

agora The marketplace in Athens.

aristocrat A member of the nobility or ruling class.

autocracy Rule by one person, such as a king, who is given absolute power over the people.

barracks A dormitory-style dwelling used to house soldiers.

chorus A group of singers and dancers that commented on the action of a Greek play.

comedy A play in which humor is used to tell a story.

courtier A servant or adviser in the court of a king.

defendant The person on trial in a court case.

democracy A political system in ancient Greece that gave each citizen of the city-state a right to vote on policies.

dialogues Discussions between two or more characters.

epic poetry Poems that tell the story of the deeds of a great hero or heroes.

ethics A system of moral values or principles.

101

forms Objects or ideas outside of human experience that can only be understood through the mind.

Helot A Spartan slave.

hemisphere Half of a sphere. The Western Hemisphere is the western half of the earth separated north to south by a division line.

hypotenuse The side opposite the right angle of a right triangle.

metics Free men who had immigrated to Athens.

metropolitan Relating to a large city or urban area.

monotheism The worship of or belief in one god.

mortal A human being.

oligarchy Government by a small group that makes policy decisions for all.

oracle A person who gives wise answers and has the ability to see into the future.

orchestra A circle of ground used by the chorus in ancient Greek theater.

paganism Worship of many gods, or religion that is not Christian, Muslim, or Jewish.

Peloponnesian War A conflict between Athens and Sparta lasting from 431 to 404 BC.

philosopher One who seeks enlightenment and loves wisdom.

philosophy The pursuit of wisdom.

piety Devotion to the gods.

platonic love Nonromantic love.

polis A city-state in ancient Greece.

polytheism The worship of or belief in more than one god.

Sophists Teachers who traveled through Greece teaching classes for a fee.

stonemason Craftsperson who works with brick or stone.

syllogism A conclusion that can be made from two different ideas that are factual.

tragedy A story about a character whose faults lead him or her to failure.

tragic flaw An insurmountable defect that leads a person to make grave mistakes.

tyrant A leader who uses his power in a cruel way.

utopia A perfect society.

For More Information

The American Classical League
Miami University
Oxford, OH 45056
Web site: http://www.aclclassics.org

The American Philosophical Association
31 Amstel Avenue
University of Delaware
Newark, DE 19716-4797
Web site: http://www.udel.edu/apa

Musée du Louvre (The Louvre)
Department of Greek, Etruscan and Roman
Antiquities
Pyramide–Cour Napoléon
75001 Paris, France
Web site: http://www.paris.org/Musees/Louvre/
    Treasures/GreekRoman

The PLATO Society of UCLA
1083 Gayley Avenue, 2nd Floor

Los Angeles, CA 90024
Web site: http://www.unex.ucla.edu/plato

The Society for the Promotion of Hellenic Studies
Senate House, Malet Street
London WC1E 7HU
England
Web site: http://www.hellenicsociety.org.uk

WEB SITES

Due to the changing nature of Internet links, the Rosen Publishing Group, Inc., has developed an online list of Web sites related to the subject of this book. This site is updated regularly. Please use this link to access the list:

http://www.rosenlinks.com/lgp/plat

FOR FURTHER READING

Guthrie, W. K. C. *The Greek Philosophers*. New York, NY: Harper & Row, 1975.

Hamilton, Edith. *The Greek Way*. New York, NY: W. W. Norton & Company, 1993.

Klein, Jacob. *A Commentary on Plato's "Meno."* Chicago, IL: University of Chicago Press, 1989.

Magee, Bryan. *The Great Philosophers*. Oxford, England: Oxford University Press, 2000.

Sowerby, Robin. *The Greeks: An Introduction to Their Culture*. Oxford, England: Routledge, 1995.

Stone, I. F. *The Trial of Socrates*. New York, NY: Anchor Books, 1989.

Zeller, Eduard. *Outlines of the History of Greek Philosophy*. New York, NY: Dover Publications, 1980.

BIBLIOGRAPHY

Baker, Rosalie F., and Charles F. Baker III, *Ancient Greeks: Creating the Classical Tradition*. Oxford, England: Oxford University Press, 1997.

Buchanan, Scott, ed. *The Portable Plato*. New York, NY: Penguin, 1977.

Cavalier, Robert. *Plato for Beginners*. New York, NY: Writers and Readers, 1998.

Freeland, Cynthia. "Ancient Greek Philosophy." University of Houston. Retrieved January 2005 (http://www.uh.edu/~cfreelan/courses/plato.html).

Loverance, Rowena, and Tim Wood. *Ancient Greece*. New York, NY: Viking, 1992.

Plato. *The Republic*. Translated by Allan Bloom. New York, NY: Basic Books, 1991.

Powell, Anton. *Cultural Atlas for Young People: Ancient Greece*. New York, NY: Facts on File, 2003.

Strathern, Paul. *Plato in 90 Minutes*. Chicago, IL: Ivan R. Dee, 1996.

Wikipedia. "Aristotle." Retrieved January 2005 (http://
en.wikipedia.org/wiki/The_Form_of_the_Good).

Wikipedia. "Plato." Retrieved January 2005 (http://
en.wikipedia.org/wiki/Plato).

INDEX

ABOUT THE AUTHOR

Alex Sniderman came to his interest in Plato and Greek philosophy from his research for this book. Mr. Sniderman's study on Plato is his first foray into following in the footsteps of his great-grandfather R. M. Wenley, who came from Scotland to be the first chairman of the philosophy department at the University of Michigan, Ann Arbor. Mr. Sniderman lives in Brooklyn, New York.

PHOTO CREDITS

Cover, title page Erich Lessing/Art Resource, NY; cover (inset), title page (inset) SEF/Art Resource, NY; pp. 7, 43 © Bettmann/Corbis; p. 10 The Metropolitan Museum of Art, Fletcher Fund, 1931 (31.11.10). Photograph © 1999 The Metropolitan Museum of Art; p. 13 akg-images/Peter Connolly; p. 16 The Art Archive/Archaeological Museum Salonica/Dagli Orti; pp. 18–19, 85 © Archivo Iconografico, S.A./Corbis; p. 21 Private Collection, Archives Charmet/Bridgeman Art Library; p. 22 © 2004 Werner Forman/Topham/The Image Works; pp. 24–25, 80–81 Originally published in Historical Atlas of the World, © J. W. Cappelens Forlag A/S, Oslo, 1962. Maps by Berit Lie. Used with permission of J. W. Cappelens Forlag; p. 25 © James P. Blair/National Geographic/Getty Images; p. 27 Ann Ronan Picture Library/HIP/ The Image Works; p. 30 Bibliothèque de la Faculté de Médecine, Paris, France, Archives Charmet/ Bridgeman Art Library; p. 32 akg-images/John Hios; p. 35 akg images/ Gilles Mermet; Biblioteca Medicea-Laurenziana, Florence,Italy/Bridgeman Art Library; p. 41 © A. Vossberg/VISUM/The Image Works; p. 49 The Art Archive/Sucevita Monastery Moldavia Romania/Dagli Orti (A); pp. 52–53, 76–77 The Vatican Library; pp. 55, 95 © The British Library/ HIP/The Image Works; p. 60 © Charles Walker/Topfoto/The Image Works; p. 63 Museé de la Chartreuse, Douai, France, Giraudon/Bridgeman Art Library; p. 67 Private Collection, Ancient Art and Architecture Collection Ltd/Bridgeman Art Library; pp.70–71 © Stapleton Collection/Corbis; pp. 74, 92 akg-images; p. 78 ÖNB, Bildarchiv, Wien; p. 79 Bibliothèque Inguimbertine, Carpentras, France/Bridgeman Art Library; p. 80 Museé Condé, Chantilly, France/Bridgeman Art Library; p.87 British Library; p. 89 Rare Book, Manuscript, and Special Collections Library, Duke University; p. 96 Scala/Art Resource, NY; p. 98 Bibliotèque Nationale, Paris, France, Flammarion/Bridgeman Art Library.

Designer: Tahara Anderson

Photo Researcher: Amy Feinberg

112